Touching His Scar

Mary McCormack

Also by Mary McCormack:

Tastes of Sunlight: Haiku for the Seasons
Brushstrokes
All the Words Kept Inside

ISBN-13: 978-0-9981720-5-7

Cover Photo & Design: Mary McCormack

Acknowledgments:

Thanks to the editors of the following journals in which these poems were first published:

Wales Haiku Journal: "wind in the reeds"
Frogpond: "returned from war"
cattails: "all his anger"

asking her
(the impossible)
not to care

Touching His Scar

war
undiluted
horror

when ruthless
meets mercy
who wins?

every moment
fighting
self-anger

bone-weary
he falls asleep
standing up

morphine--
letting the river
sweep him away

rage
finding nowhere to go
the mole burrows deeper

scared
beyond
the imaginable

pulled taut
all his anger
in that one word

hatred…
so many layers
of sediment

hardened
by all this
anger

going to war
means never coming back
the same

more than tragedy can contain

so many graves...
and untold stories
of war

waves...
everything washed away
but the guilt

returned from war
the only one he talks to
his tiny niece

up before dawn
the sound
of his thoughts

remembering
them
before

the places he goes
in his mind
that no one else knows

sometimes lonelier
with people
than without

never possible
to tell
the whole story

guilt...
an unshakable
partner

running his fingers
over their names
on the gravestones

in his thoughts
they're as alive now
as they were then

seizing him
from the inside
hurt

no one knows
until it's over
how changed they'll be

through windows
the glow of warmth
lonely night

a long road
through withered fields
the mourning dove's cry

at your most miserable
can you care about
another's misery?

loneliness
an endless well
to draw from

feeling (a)part (fr)o(m)f everything

a silver droplet
on the clover leaf
shivers

last night's rain
shaken loose from the oak
old griefs

wind in the reeds
long after their deaths
ripples

sorry...
not enough weight
to that word

her
hand
touching
his
scar

About the Author:

Mary McCormack is a writer and teacher of poetry, fiction, and nonfiction. Her haiku have been widely published in the US and internationally.

Website: www.marymwriter.com